How to Become a Black Cat and Get Your Golden Retriever

From Meow to Wow: Capturing His Heart with Black Cat Confidence

Author: Isla Bratt

CONTENTS

Introduction

How to Become a Black Cat and Get Your Golden Retriever

If you're ready to take your relationships to the next level and make a man adore you while putting yourself first, you've come to the right place.

This book is your ultimate guide to embracing your inner black cat - confident, independent, sassy and irresistibly mysterious.

Your journey begins

In these pages, you'll find practical tips, inspiring quotes from experts and fun exercises designed to help you charm, tease and keep the spark alive. You'll learn how to balance your independence with your romantic life, dress to impress, and master the art of the flirt.

Being a black cat means owning who you are, setting high standards, and never apologizing for your fabulousness. It's about knowing your worth and making him work for your affection. After all, a black cat doesn't chase; she attracts.

Get ready to transform yourself and your relationships. It's time to unleash your inner black cat and have your golden retriever (man) wagging his tail in adoration.

Chapter 1: Embrace Your Inner Black Cat

2. Confidence is key

Confidence doesn't mean arrogance! It's about knowing your worth and not settling for less. It's the silent, steady assurance that you are enough just as you are. This confidence is built over time through self-reflection, self-love, and practice.

Start by practicing positive affirmations daily. Stand tall with good posture, make eye contact, and smile. Engage in activities that make you feel accomplished and proud, whether it's working out, learning a new skill, or pursuing a passion. Confidence is magnetic; it draws people in and makes them want to be around you.

3

Practice confidence

Practice positive affirmations every morning, for example:

"I am worthy of love and respect"

Use a power pose, such as standing with your hands on your hips like Wonder Woman, for two minutes before a big event to boost your confidence.

Additionally, keep a journal where you list your daily accomplishments and things you're grateful for. This practice reinforces your self-worth and boosts your confidence.

"Confidence isn't about being perfect; its about being authentic. Own who you are and others will naturally be drawn to your energy."

Sarah J.
Career Coach

Stand in front of a mirror every morning and say five positive things about yourself out loud to build confidence. This helps you start your day in a black cat manner.

- I am healthy
- I am lucky
- I love and accept my body
- My mind is clear and focused
- All I need is within me
- I can do anything
- People love to be around me
- I embrace new possibilities
- Adventure comes to me easily
- I attract a good men
- Everything always works out in my favour

2. Mystery is attractive

Don't spill all your secrets at once. Keep some aspects of your life private and reveal them slowly. This keeps him intrigued and wanting to know more. Mystery is an essential component of attraction because it creates an aura of allure and fascination. It's not about being secretive or dishonest but about maintaining an element of surprise and depth. Share bits of your life and experiences gradually, allowing him to uncover different layers of your personality over time. This gradual revelation keeps the excitement and curiosity alive, making the relationship more dynamic and engaging.

Also, maintain your private time and space. It's important to have parts of your life that are solely yours, whether it's a hobby, a personal goal, or time with friends. This not only keeps you grounded but also adds to your allure.

Share a story about your hobbies or interests in stages. For example, if you love painting, mention it casually and then invite him to a gallery exhibit you're part of or show him one of your works after a few dates. Or, if you're into traveling, share your favorite travel stories one at a time, leaving him eager to hear more about your adventures.

"Mystery creates a desire to understand. Reveal yourself gradually and let him discover you layer by layer."

Emily R.,
Relationship Expert

Practise mystery

Tell him through your energy and attitude that there are many things about you that he doesn´t know yet.

Write down five things about yourself that you don't usually share with new people. Keep these as little secrets to reveal over time.

Learn how to regulate your nervous system so that you can keep your cool in every situation. When you react strongly to what other people say or do you give away your power. A black cat always stays unbothered, even if she is boiling on the inside.

3. Own Your Independence

Men are intrigued by women who are a mental challenge to them. If your energy is unatainable and almost untouchable he will be lured in and commit to you. Have your own hobbies, interests, and social circle. Independence is sexy because it shows you are self-sufficient and fulfilled on your own.

Being independent means you have a life outside the relationship, which prevents you from becoming overly reliant on your partner for happiness and validation. It demonstrates that you value yourself and your time, and it encourages a healthier, more balanced relationship dynamic.

Engage in activities that you love and make time for your friends and family. Pursue your goals and dreams with passion. When you are fulfilled and happy on your own, you bring a richer, more vibrant version of yourself to the relationship. This independence also sets boundaries, showing that while you cherish your partner, you also cherish your individuality.

Create a "Me Time" schedule where you dedicate time each week to pursue your hobbies, catch up with friends, and engage in activities that you love without him. For instance, join a club or class that interests you, spend a weekend on a solo trip, or have a regular girls' night out. These activities will not only enrich your life but also keep the relationship balanced.

"Independence is a superpower. When you have your own goals and ambitions, you become unstoppable and incredibly attractive."

Linda K.
Entrepreneur

Practise independence

Create a weekly plan that includes time for your own interests and social activities without your partner. This helps you build and maintain your own identity.

Do not always be available for at date. Say no sometimes. Your time is valuable.

Don´t always reach out first or pick up every single phone call. Be to busy sometimes and call back later.

Reflect regularly on your core values. Journalling is a great way to do this.

Keep hanging out with your friends without him. This is important!

Set and always keep your boundaries. They are non negotiable and your man will test them.

Chapter 2: The Art of Tease and Please

4. Master the Flirt

Flirting is an art. It's about subtle touches, playful banter, and light teasing. The key is to be genuine and have fun. Flirting isn't just about the initial attraction; it's also a way to keep the romance alive in an established relationship. Use body language to your advantage - lean in slightly when he's talking, play with your hair, or lightly touch his arm during conversation. Playful banter is also essential. Tease him lightly about something he said or did in a way that shows you're paying attention and that you enjoy his company. The goal is to create a lighthearted, fun atmosphere that both of you enjoy.

Remember, the best flirting is sincere and comes from a place of genuine interest and enjoyment.

Use playful teasing in conversation. For instance, if he says something funny, lightly touch his arm and say, "Oh, you think you're so clever, don't you?" followed by a smile. Or, if he shares a childhood story, playfully respond with, "I bet you were a handful back then!" This kind of banter keeps the conversation lively and engaging.

Both men and women love a good sense of humor. There is nothing more bonding than sharing a joke together. A private joke between the two of you can last for months, even years. And it's yours and only yours.

A black cat is sassy, fun and confident when she flirts. But at the same time deep and thoughtful.

Black cat´s guide to flirting

1. Have fun!
2. Be yourself
3. Ask thoughtful questions
4. Open up about yourself too
5. Make eye contact and keep it
6. Use subtle boudy language
7. Smile across the room
8. Be honest and straight forward
9. Suggest hanging out in a group
10. Send smile-worthy texts
11. Include humor in your chats
12. Go with the flow of the conversation
13. Be playful
14. Handle the situation with respect
15. Engage with kindness and empathy
16. Be totally present
17. Build a connection with common ground
18. Remember, flirting is a two-way-street

"Flirting is about creating a playful energy. Its not about being perfect; its about being present and having fun."

James T.
Dating Coach

Practise flirting

Practice giving compliments and smiling more often. Notice how people react to your positivity and use this as a foundation to develop your flirting skills.

Create a couple of signature lines that he learns to associate with you. Now, everytime he hears or sees it - he will think of you!

Talk in front of the mirror. Listen to your own tone of voice. Try different styles and lines. You need to be comfortable saying it to yourself if you´re gonna say it to man.

Make mental notes about current events that interest you. That way you´ll always have things to talk about, while appearing up to date.

5. Balance Availability

Don't drop everything for him. Make plans with friends, pursue your interests, and let him see that you have a fulfilling life outside of the relationship. Being too available can sometimes make you appear less desirable or needy. Instead, maintain a healthy balance where you have your own life and also make time for him.

This balance shows that you value your own time and interests while also valuing the relationship. It creates a sense of anticipation and excitement when you do spend time together. Communicate your schedule clearly and stick to it. This not only respects your time but also sets a standard for how you expect to be treated. A man should always be the one pursuing you, but not with a 100 per cent sucess rate.

Plan a week where you have specific times set aside for your activities and social engagements. Communicate your schedule to him so he knows when you're available. For example, let him know you're free after your yoga class on Wednesday or after your book club meeting on Friday. This way, he understands that you have commitments and interests outside the relationship.

It´s always a good idea to plant seeds with men, and never a good idea to be nagging... Tell him about a restaurant you want to visit, that you love getting flowers or really like miniature golfing. And then pay attention to if he´s paying attention. Does he listen to you? Care about what you are saying? If so, he will book the restaurant, bring flowers and take you golfing after dinner.

"Healthy relationships thrive on balance. Being too available can create dependency, while having your own life fosters mutual respect."

Dr. Amanda F.
Psychologist

Practise balanced availability

Create a diary where you write down your plans and activities. This helps you keep track of your own time and ensures you are not always available.

Always prioritize taking care of your body and soul. What makes you thrive? Going to the gym? Deep breathing? Taking a walk in nature? An hour on the yoga mat? Meditation? Affirmations?

What ever it is - do that consistently. Healthy relationships come from healthy people. When you feel good about yourself, you can give your time and energy to others.

When ever you´re about to do something, always ask yourself: "Is this good for my health? Is this benefiting my future?"

6. Charm with Wit

Engage in intelligent conversation. He will love that! Use humor to your advantage. Witty exchanges can create a deeper connection and show off your personality. Wit is a sign of intelligence and creativity. It shows that you can think on your feet and enjoy mental sparring. Share interesting facts, clever observations, or funny anecdotes.

Ask open-ended questions that encourage deeper conversation and demonstrate your interest in his thoughts and opinions. Use humor to lighten the mood and create a relaxed, enjoyable atmosphere. Remember, charm isn't about trying to impress him; it's about being your authentic, delightful self.

Challenge him to a playful debate on a light topic, such as "Which is better: beach vacations or mountain getaways?" Use humor and logic to keep the conversation lively. Share funny stories from your own experiences to illustrate your points and keep the conversation engaging.

Play battle-of-movie-quotes where you challenge each other with fun and witty one-liners from your favourite movies.

From the movie Jackie Brown, 1997
Jackie Brown walks into a bar. She is looking for someone and walks up to the bartender. They chit chat for a while and engage in light flirting.

Bartender: Can I get you anything?
Jackie Brown: No thanks, I´m fine.
Bartender: Yes you are....

Wit is the spice of life. It shows intelligence and keeps conversations interesting."

Laura B.
Stand-up
Comedian

Practise your wit

The easiest way to become witty is to associate with witty people. A black cat knows her strengths and can make people laugh just through being intelligent, sassy and up to date.

1. Relax and let loose
2. Acquire more knowledge
3. Use the element of surprise
4. Do your homework
5. Be present in the moment
6. Appear more friendly
7. Believe in yourself
8. Never put people down
9. Remember good jokes
10. Take more risks
11. Learn from funny people
12. Know when to stop

Chapter 3: The Power of Physical Attraction

7. Dress to Impress

Your style reflects your personality. Dress in a way that makes you feel confident and attractive. Invest in pieces that highlight your best features. Fashion is a form of self-expression. It's not about following trends but about finding what makes you feel your best. Experiment with different styles and colors to discover what suits you. Pay attention to the details, like how well your clothes fit and how they make you feel. When you dress to impress, you're not just looking good for others; you're boosting your own confidence and sense of self-worth. Also, consider the occasion and dress appropriately, balancing comfort with style.

Remember, the way you present yourself can greatly influence how others perceive you.

Create a capsule wardrobe with versatile pieces that can be dressed up or down. Include a list of must-have items like a little black dress, tailored blazer, and comfortable yet stylish shoes. Invest in a few high-quality pieces that you can mix and match to create different looks. Pay attention to how different colors and styles make you feel, and choose outfits that boost your confidence.

Men are visual beings. The first thing they will notice about you is how you look and present yourself, and radiance comes from feeling good. It´s not the most beautiful woman that keeps a man interested, but the woman who feels good about herself, which will reflect on her appearence. Feel good, look good!

"Your style is a reflection of your personality. Dress in a way that makes you feel confident and you'll naturally attract positive attention."

Marie L.
Fashion Stylist

Practise style

Create a mood board with clothing styles and accessories that inspire you. Use this as a guide when shopping for new clothes and accessories.

It´s important to know your colors and coordinate them. Using the right colors has a huge impact on your radiance. If possible, do a professional color analysis.

It´s also a good idea to invest in timeless neutral pieces, instead of following trends. Classic, timeless pieces never go out of style and buying them is one of the best investments you can make.

Be objective about your body shape. Emphasize your best parts. Accept who you are today. Become attuned to what you like and don't like. Listen to when others compliment you, and make notice!

8. Sensuality Matters

Sensuality is about engaging all the senses. Use fragrances, soft fabrics, and touch to create an alluring atmosphere. Sensuality goes beyond physical appearance; it's about creating an experience that appeals to all the senses. Choose fragrances that make you feel confident and attractive. Soft, comfortable fabrics can enhance your physical presence and make you feel more at ease.

Pay attention to the textures and colors that you surround yourself with, whether it's in your clothing, your home decor, or your personal care products. Create a sensory-rich environment that makes you feel relaxed and desirable. Sensuality is also about the way you move and carry yourself. Slow down, be mindful of your movements, and engage fully with your surroundings.

Sensuality is triggered by anything that makes you feel physically good and makes your entire being calm. This can range from soothing music, good food, lovely reads, sunsets, nature walks. etc. The essential driving factors toward being sensual are self-love and self-worth.

Experiment with different fragrances and find one that makes you feel confident and sexy. Use scented candles or essential oils in your living space to create a welcoming and sensual environment. Wear fabrics that feel good against your skin, like silk or cashmere. Pay attention to your grooming and self-care routines, using products that enhance your sensory experience.

And last but not least. Always own your sexuality by knowing your likes and boundaries. There is nothing sexier than a woman who knows how to communicate what she desires. 33

"Engage all your senses to create a memorable presence. Scent, touch, and sight all play a crucial role in attraction."

Nina M.
Aromatherapist

Practice sensuality

1. Love your body
Loving your body is the most critical step to becoming sensual.

2. Be kind to yourself
Sensuality encompasses self-love and adornment.

3. Meditate
It's in silent meditation that you entirely get in touch with your spiritual and emotional self.

4. Embrace a self-love ritual
Self-care and pampering is the ultimate expression of loving your body.

5. Be mindful
Deliberately take note of everything that happens around you. Pay attention to sounds, nature, and beautiful sights.

9. Eye Contact is Everything

Eyes are windows to the soul. Use eye contact to show interest, convey emotions, and create a connection. Eye contact is a powerful form of nonverbal communication. It can convey confidence, interest, and sincerity. When you make eye contact, you show that you are fully present and engaged in the moment. It helps build trust and intimacy.

Practice making eye contact in a relaxed and natural way. Avoid staring, which can be intimidating, but don't be afraid to hold someone's gaze for a few seconds longer than usual. This shows that you are confident and interested. Use your eyes to express your emotions, whether it's joy, curiosity, or affection. Eye contact can also be a form of flirting. A playful glance, a slow blink, or a subtle wink can all convey interest and attraction.

Practice making and maintaining eye contact in a mirror. Notice how your eyes can express different emotions like curiosity, interest, and affection. Use this technique in conversations to build a deeper connection.

When you're talking to someone, try to hold their gaze for a few seconds longer than usual, then look away and back again. This creates a sense of intimacy and connection. In fact, eye contact is way more intimate than words or sex can ever be.

I still remember the day
When our eyes first acquainted
A trivial moment of almost nothing
And yet the timeless beginning
of everything

Timothy Joshua

"Eye contact builds trust and intimacy. It's a silent way of saying 'I'm here with you, fully present."

David H.
Communication Expert

Practice eye contact

Practice maintaining eye contact for short periods with people you meet daily. Gradually increase the time to build up your comfort level.

Every 4-5 seconds, focus on a different spot on someone's face - their eyes and mouth, for example - to avoid feeling like you're staring and to maintain and interested appearance. Practice at home. You don't need another person to practice eye contact.

Apply the 50/70 rule: Aim to make eye contact 50% of the time when you speak and 70% of the time when you listen.

If a person makes gestures when they are speaking, they are telling the truth. If they are still, their energy is needed for making up stories in their head...

Chapter 4: Emotional Intelligence

10. Listen and Respond

Active listening shows you care. It's about giving your full attention, asking questions, and responding thoughtfully. Listening is a fundamental aspect of communication and connection. When you listen actively, you demonstrate that you value the other person's thoughts and feelings. It involves more than just hearing the words; it's about understanding the underlying emotions and intentions.

Practice active listening by nodding, maintaining eye contact, and providing feedback. Ask open-ended questions that encourage the other person to elaborate. Show empathy by acknowledging their feelings and perspectives.

Respond thoughtfully, taking the time to consider your words before speaking. Active listening helps build trust and intimacy, making the other person feel valued and understood.

Use active listening techniques such as nodding, paraphrasing what he said, and asking follow-up questions. For example, "So what you're saying is...?" or "That sounds really interesting, tell me more about..." This shows that you are paying attention and encourages deeper conversation.

Remember, listening is one of the most important aspects of communication. Successful listening is not just about understanding what the other person is saying, but also an understanding of how the they feel during communication.

"Listening is an art. Its about being fully present and making the other person feel heard and valued."

Dr. Sylvia P. Therapist

Practise listening

Have an "active listening" session with a friend. Practice paraphrasing what they say and asking follow-up questions to show that you are listening attentively.

- Be fully present and attentive
- Use positive body language and nonverbal cues
- Avoid interrupting or judging
- Paraphrase and reflect to show understanding
- Ask clarifying and open-ended questions
- Validate their perspective and emotions
- Withhold advice unless asked
- Summarize key points and action item

11. Be Supportive but not Overbearing

Support his dreams and goals without trying to control or direct him. Encourage him and be his cheerleader. Supporting your partner means believing in their abilities and offering encouragement and assistance when needed. It's important to be a source of positive energy and motivation. However, it's equally important to give him space to pursue his goals independently.

Avoid being overbearing or controlling, which can create resentment and dependency. Offer your help and support, but respect his autonomy. Celebrate his achievements and be there for him during setbacks. A supportive partner fosters a healthy, balanced relationship where both individuals feel valued and empowered.

When he talks about his goals, offer specific encouragement. Say something like, "I believe in you and know you can achieve this," and ask how you can support him without taking over. Show interest in his progress and celebrate his milestones, no matter how small. Checking in regularly on his progress and helping him overcome any challenges that come up is also crucial.

A friendly way to help him come closer to his goals, without turning into his mother:

1. Ask about his goals
2. Listen without giving advice
3. Set reminders to check in
4. Offer him accountability
5. Offer your help

Remember - he is always responsible for the way his life is going, but there is nothing wrong with being supportive!

"Support means believing in their dreams while giving them space to achieve them. Its about partnership, not ownership."

Tom R.
Life Coach

Practise support

Write down three ways you can support your partner without being overbearing. Discuss these with your partner and agree on how you can best support each other.

Individual Reflection
Take some quiet time to reflect on the ways you currently support your partner.
Writing Down Your Support Strategies
Clearly articulate three ways you can support your partner.
Discussion
Arrange a time when both you and your partner can sit down without distractions.
Agreeing on Mutual Support
Together, decide on the best ways you can support each other, ensuring that both of you feel valued and respected.
Implementation and Reflection
Put your agreed-upon support strategies into practice. Check in with each other regularly.

47

12. Handle Conflicts Gracefully

Disagreements are natural. It's how you handle them that matters. Stay calm, listen to his perspective, and communicate your feelings clearly. Conflict is a normal part of any relationship, but it doesn't have to be destructive. Approach conflicts with a calm and open mind. Avoid getting defensive or resorting to personal attacks.

Instead, focus on the issue at hand and express your feelings using "I" statements, such as "I feel..." or "I need..." Listen to his perspective without interrupting, and acknowledge his feelings and viewpoints. Look for common ground and work together to find a resolution that satisfies both parties. Handling conflicts gracefully strengthens the relationship and builds mutual respect and understanding.

For example, if you disagree about how to spend your weekends, suggest alternating activities to ensure both of your preferences are respected.

However ladies! Remember that the black cat always keeps her cool. She stays unbothered in every situation, so that no one can have power over her.

- If he wants to go out with the boys - let him
- If he´s following beautiful women on Instagram - whatever
- If he scrolls on his phone - fine

Men learn through action, not words. Do not nag, but instead remove yourself from the situation. He will notice that you´re gone and come chasing after you because men always compete with their own ego.

"Conflict is inevitable, but its also an opportunity for growth. Handle it with grace and empathy and you'll build a stronger bond."

Anna S.
Conflict Resolution Expert

Practice healthy conflict

When a conflict arises, take a moment to breathe and calm yourself. Use "I feel" statements instead of "You did" statements to express your emotions without blaming the other person.

The Five Steps to Conflict Resolution

- Step 1: Identify the source of the conflict. The more information about the cause of the conflict, the more easily it can be resolved
- Step 2: Look beyond the incident
- Step 3: Request solutions
- Step 4: Identify solutions you both can support
- Step 5: Agreement

Chapter five: The Formula on How to Become a Black Cat

A work in progress

Be noticeable. A black cat always strives to be sexy, seductive, hot and powerful, rather then being cute, bubbly, nice and pretty. This high value woman makes heads turn and change the frequency and energy of the room as soon as she walks in.

Be seductive. Let your body speak before you even open your mouth. Open your shoulders, show your neck, give people a smile and withhold eye contact. Confident women are not scared of being noticed.

Be calm. Take things slow. Calm people radiance confidence. Why? Because they know they have something that other people want. Coolness. These are the people that usually get their way in the end. People are drawn to the black cat because they want to solve the mystery that they are. Loud people get attention, but it´s very short lived.

Talk less. Paus and hold space so that other people can come your way. In business, families and relationships the person who speaks less always wins.

Go slow. Confident, sexy women are slow. Being in your feminine energy means to be soft, slow and able to surrender. This energy is not only radiating femininity, but also high class. There is no chaos or drama, only self confidence.

53

BLACK CATS
DOS AND DON'TS

DON'T	DO
Depend on him	Stay independant
Chase him	Let him chase you
Try to prove yourself to him by doing so much	Realize you are the prize. That's enough!
Sit at home waiting for him when he's out	Go out and have fun with the girls
Compete with other women	Stay unbothered, you know you are the best
Put all your focus and attention on him	Always put yourself first
Be clingy or needy	Be self-reliant
Accept last minutes plans	Decline. Go elsewhere
Put up with bad behaviour	Withdraw and set clear boundaries

The psychology of men

Ladies, let's be real: men are simple creatures. Understanding their psychology can give you the upper hand in any relationship. If you want a man to value, appreciate, and spoil you, you've got to tap into his instinct to protect and provide.

Here's the deal: constantly telling him what to do and trying to control his actions will only trigger his competitive side. This leads to resentment, and soon enough, he'll stop doing all those sweet things he did in the beginning. Men don't want to feel overshadowed by their partner. Yes, let him wear the pants!

Men are always competing for women's attention. Whether it's career, clothes, Instagram posts, jokes, muscles, money, or the car that they drive, it's all about impressing the ladies.

For men, status and influence surpass physical appearance, though they know the value of looking good too.

A man won't respect your words if your actions don't match. Bad behavior from him should always be met with you pulling back and withdrawing your time and attention. As a black cat, your absence is your greatest leverage. Be a pleasure to be around, so every time you pull back, he starts craving you more.

Make him feel like a man. Compliment him, satisfy his ego, and be feminine and playful. But here's the kicker: only give him limited access to this side of you. Everyone wants what they can't easily have.

Lastly, men fear rejection like nothing else. Sometimes they settle for their second choice just to avoid the heartbreak of losing the woman they truly love. You are the prize. That's enough! Stop overdoing it and let him chase you.

A good man holds himself accountable, takes responsibility for his actions, does what is right regardless of the popularity, maintains the highest integrity and harbors values and respect for all.

He does not ever lie, cheat, make excuses or blame you when things go wrong. If you ever encouter that type of weak man, leave and never look back.

Remember! You deserve the best and are willing to wait for it. A golden retriever is loyal, mentally strong and more than proud to be with his black cat.

"A good man loves to show off his happy, intelligent, amazing, radiant woman."

Summary: Own Your Fabulousness

Congratulations! You've journeyed through the art of becoming a black cat and securing your golden retriever. You've learned to exude confidence, maintain a touch of mystery, and balance your independence with your romantic life. You've mastered flirting, dressing to impress, and engaging in intelligent conversations. You've discovered the power of sensuality, eye contact, and emotional intelligence.

Remember, being a black cat means prioritizing yourself, embracing your unique qualities, and never settling for less than you deserve, a good and loyal man/golden retriever.

xoxo

Made in United States
North Haven, CT
27 November 2024

61102200R10035